West Virginia Real Estate Salesperson Exam

"You never fail until you stop trying" - Albert Einstein

For inquiries;
info@xmprep.com

West Virginia Real Estate Salesperson Exam #1

Test Taking Tips

☐ Take a deep breath and relax

☐ Read directions carefully

☐ Read the questions thoroughly

☐ Make sure you understand what is being asked

☐ Go over all of the choices before you answer

☐ Paraphrase the question

☐ Eliminate the options you know are wrong

☐ Check your work

☐ Think positively and do your best

Table of Contents

TEST DIRECTION

DIRECTIONS

Read the questions carefully and then choose the ONE best answer to each question.

Be sure to allocate your time carefully so you are able to complete the entire test within the testing session. You may go back and review your answers at any time.

You may use any available space in your test booklet for scratch work.

Questions in this booklet are not actual test questions but they are the samples for commonly asked questions.

This test aims to cover all topics which may appear on the actual test. However some topics may not be covered.

Studying this booklet will be preparing you for the actual test. It will not guarantee improving your test score but it will help you pass your exam on the first attempt.

Some useful tips for answering multiple choice questions;

- Start with the questions that you can easily answer.

- Underline the keywords in the question.

- Be sure to read all the choices given.

- Watch for keywords such as NOT, always, only, all, never, completely.

- Do not forget to answer every question.

1

Joint tenancy refers to the holding of an estate or property jointly by two or more parties, the share of each passing to the other or others on death.

Which of the following should other joint tenants do upon the death of a joint tenant?

A) Share the deceased tenant's share equally.
B) Share the property with the spouse of the deceased joint tenant.
C) Duke it out in the lawyer's office
D) Must go to court for a disposition of the matter

2

A **covenant**, in real property law, is used for conditions tied to the use of land.

Which of the following enforces a covenant in a deed?

A) Local police
B) Court order
C) Habendum clause
D) The condo association

3

Building foundation supports a building from underneath.

Which of the following is the material that is most commonly used for foundations?

A) Concrete
B) Steel
C) PVC
D) Wood

2

CONTINUE ▶

4

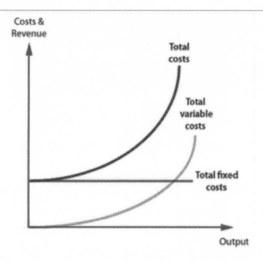

Costs & Revenue

Total costs

Total variable costs

Total fixed costs

Output

Variable cost refers to an expense that varies with production output. Variable costs are those costs that vary depending on volume; they rise as production increases and fall as production decreases. Variable costs differ from fixed costs.

Which of the following is most likely a variable expense?

A) Heating fuel

B) License fees

C) Taxes

D) None of the above

5

Which of the following is the result of the death of a landlord?

A) Cheers and cartwheels

B) Termination of the lease

C) Automatic renewal of the lease

D) Indefinite extension of the lease

6

The **Civil Rights Act of 1866** explains citizenship and affirms that the law equally protects all citizens.

Which of the following refers to the basis for the Civil Rights Act of 1866 that prohibits discrimination without exception?

A) National Origin

B) Religion

C) Race

D) All of the above

CONTINUE ▶

7

A Mortgage Broker, specializing in real estate transactions, acts as the middleman between a client (a person or a company) and a specific bank.

The client's financial ability to pay a potential mortagage is reviewed to decide if the client is financially established for the bank to back their real estate purchase.

Which of the following mostly involves a mortgage broker?

A) Property value determination
B) Originating loan applications
C) Providing the mortgage loan funds
D) All of the above

8

Obtaining a mortgage is an essential part of the buying process, while securing mortgage pre-qualification and pre-approval are necessary steps, assuring lenders that you'll be able to afford payments.

Which of the following can a pre-approval letter substitute?

A) Agent qualifying
B) State disclosure form
C) Mortgage commitment
D) Lead-based paint disclosure

CONTINUE ▶

Property tax is an assessed real estate tax which is usually based on the value of the property owned and is often evaluated by local or municipal governments. It is a primary source of revenue for many local governments.

Which of the following about property tax is not correct?

A) It is a real estate ad-valorem tax, calculated by a local government, which is paid by the owner of the property.

B) It is usually based on the value of the owned property, including land.

C) Millage rate is the other name given to property tax.

D) Property classes, tax rates, assessment rules and valuations are constant and do not vary by jurisdiction.

Wetlands are the areas where the water covers the soil for varying periods of time during the year and supports both aquatic and terrestrial species.

The existence of water creates favorable conditions for growth of specially adapted plants (hydrophytes) and promotes the development of characteristic wetland (hydric) soils.

Which of the following department is involved in a wetland's possible development?

A) Conservation Advisory Council

B) Town Council

C) Landmark Preservation Commission

D) Planning Board

11

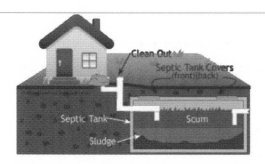

A **septic tank** is a type of watertight chamber usually made of concrete, fibreglass, PVC or plastic, through which domestic wastewater (sewage) flows for primary treatment. The treated liquid effluent is commonly disposed in a septic drain field which provides further treatment.

Which of the following is the percentage of American homes having septic systems?

A) 5%

B) 10%

C) 15%

D) 25%

12

"Time is of the Essence" is used as a phrase in a contract referring to the performance by a party at or within the period specified in the contract. Failure to perform within the required time constitutes a breIt drops from the contractach in the contract.

Which of the following happens to the closing date when "time is of the essence" is invoked?

A) It becomes significant

B) It loses its importance

C) It drops from the contract

D) None of the above

13

Special assessment designates a unique charge in which government units can assess against real estate parcels for specific public projects.

Who pays special assessment?

A) All residents of the community

B) All property owners in the community

C) Only those property owners that will experience a benefit from the assessment

D) None of the above

14

Adam had an insurance plan but he has a loss. Which of the following describes a portion of the loss that is not covered?

A) Allowable

B) Deductible

C) Insurable

D) Refundable

CONTINUE ▶

15

Which of the following choices below is the best description of a condominium (usually known as a condo)?

A) Special form of cooperative ownership

B) Special form of condominium ownership

C) Special form of residential and commercial ownership

D) Special form of cooperative and condominium ownership

16

A **fiduciary** is a person who acts on behalf of another person, or persons, to manage assets. When acting as an Agent, real estate brokers and salespersons are defined as fiduciaries. They owe **undivided loyalty** to homeowners which prohibits the agents from advancing any interests adverse to their client or conducting their client's business to benefit themselves or others.

Which of the following people is undivided loyalty for?

A) Agent

B) Customer

C) Client

D) Broker

17

Property taxes in USA are mostly based on which of the following basis?

A) Ad Valorem basis

B) In-rem basis

C) Municipal basis

D) Special assessment basis

18

A **sales agent** is an authorized individual who distributes or sells products in a specific area or region.

Which of the following may compensate a sales agent?

A) His/Her seller

B) His/Her Customer

C) His/Her own broker

D) Listing agent

19

Multifamily residential refers to a type of housing where several separate residential units are within one building or several buildings within one complex.

Which of the following is a disadvantage of owning a multi-family housing?

A) Generally, there are less potential buyers for units in multi-family properties.

B) The owner may be able to avoid commercial financing if he or she lives in one of the units.

C) A vacancy in one unit would not eliminate income flow from the property.

D) Owners may receive multiple rent checks each month.

20

A **lien** refers to a claim against the property for an owed unpaid amount. A property that has a lien attached to it cannot be sold or refinanced until the taxes are paid, and the lien is removed.

Which of the following has higher priority than real estate tax lien?

A) Private liens

B) Personal liens

C) Commercial liens

D) None of the above

21

A **rate lock** is a charge set by the lender for the borrower to pay if he or she has not locked the interest rate.

Which of the following refers to a rate lock?

A) It is a part of the loan application

B) It is negotiated between the lender and borrower

C) It is installed on the front door of the property under mortgage review

D) It is generally a two-year commitment

22

Real estate property is often owned by business interests.

Which of the following about the formation of business interest is not correct?

A) Partnership is a business arrangement between two or more person or entity.

B) Joint venture is a method of pooling investors of equal interests in a real estate.

C) Cooperative is a type of corporate ownership of real property where stockholders of the corporation are entitled to certain dwellings.

D) Association is the elected governing body which is responsible for maintaining condominium property.

23

An **asset base** is the underlying assets that give value to a company, investment or loan.

Which of the following refers to a basis whereby an asset is depreciated at the same amount in each accounting period?

A) Short-term basis

B) Straight line basis

C) Deductible basis

D) None of the above

24

Multifamily residential refers to multiple separate housing units for residential inhabitants contained in one building or several buildings within one complex.

Which of the following appraisal approaches would appraise multifamily apartment building?

A) Cost

B) Income approach

C) Market data

D) All of the above

25

An **equalization factor** is used as a multiplier to assess the value of a property to get a value for the property that is in line with statewide tax assessments.

When is an equalization factor needed?

A) When commercial and residential properties need to be taxed at different tax rates.

B) When multiple communities contribute to a regional high school.

C) When a major company contributes most of the community's tax revenue.

D) When senior citizens are deserving of a lower tax rate.

26

A **community** describes a group of people living in the same place or having a particular characteristic in common.

Which of the following should a board create to develop a community?

A) Architectural review board

B) Board of trustees

C) Building department

D) Master plan

9

CONTINUE ▶

27

Which of the following is the annual taxes on a property with an assessed value of $840,000 and a tax rate of $2.05 per thousand dollars of assessed value?

A) $1,722
B) $2,100
C) $336,000
D) $409,000

28

Installment sale contract refers to the method of sale allowing for partial deferral of capital gain to any future taxation years.

In an installment sale contract on a property, when is the title conveyed to the purchaser?

A) When the full down payment has been turned over to the seller's attorney
B) At the end of the rescission period
C) When the contract is signed
D) When the last payment has been turned over to the seller

29

Which of the following could result in the cancellation of a policy by an insurer?

A) Termite infestation
B) Non-payment of premiums
C) Incapacity of a co-owner
D) Property damage

30

The government has the right to arrest and imprison any suspicious individual on the basis of rightful State Laws.

Which of the following does this situation correspond to?

A) Escheat
B) Eminent Domain
C) Police Power
D) None of the above

31

Which of the following refers to the document whereby a purchaser of property personally obligates herself to the lender?

A) Bond
B) Deed
C) Mortgage
D) Power of Attorney

32

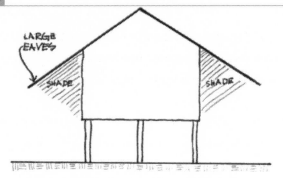

Which of the following describes the eaves of a structure in the portions of the roof?

A) Allow the attic spaces to breathe
B) Come together at the peak
C) Overhang the sides
D) None of the above

33

Deed restrictions are the type of private agreements that restrict the use of a real estate in some way which are listed in the deed. The seller may add restrictions to the title of the property. Often, developers restrict the parcels of property in a development to maintain a certain amount of uniformity.

A deed restriction is invalid if it restricts which of the following?

A) Raise cows
B) Grow crops
C) Install an outside garage
D) Sell the property

34

Which of the following refers to the heavy wooden members that sit atop the foundation wall and where the frame is placed?

A) Bridging
B) Girders
C) Joists
D) Sills

35

A **security deposit** is a monetary lump sum which is held in trust from a party as an initial part-payment in a purchasing process. It is often used to prevent the seller from selling an item to someone else during an agreed period of time while the buyer verifies the suitability of the item, or arranges finance.

In which of the following cases will the security deposits be maintained by a landlord?

A) To force a renewal of the lease by the tenant
B) In the event a fire destroys the building
C) To keep tenants from moving out before the lease is up
D) To be used to repair damage to the unit above and beyond normal wear and tear

36

A **clause** is an accord that a property owner creates with a real estate broker, saying the owner will pay the broker to lease or sell a property for a given price. It can be found in a listing agreement. An automatic extension makes the listing agreement persist after it expires, for a specified time.

Which of the following best describes the use of automatic extensions of time on listing agreements?

A) A good business practice
B) Unethical
C) It is illegal
D) None of the above

37

When a property manager prepares an operating statement, which of the following is it usually based on?

A) Weekly basis
B) Bi-monthly basis
C) Monthly basis
D) Quarterly basis

38

A **Planning and Zoning Commission** refers to a locally elected or appointed government board that is charged with making recommendations to the local town or city council about the boundaries of the various original zoning district and the appropriate regulations to be enforced.

To dispute a decision of the planning board, to which of the following should a citizen go?

A) Architectural review board
B) Building inspector
C) Ombudsman
D) Zoning board of appeals

39

Jones v. Alfred H. **Mayer** Co., 392 U.S. 409 (1968), is a landmark United States Supreme Court case, which held that Congress could regulate the sale of private property to prevent racial discrimination.

Which of the following provisions does the Jones v. Mayer Decision uphold?

A) Article 12A

B) Federal Fair Housing Act of 1968

C) New York State Executive Law

D) Civil Rights Act of 1866

40

PITI refers to a mortgage payment which is the total of monthly principal, interest, taxes, and insurance.

Which of the following would a borrower with a weekly income of $2,350 qualify for a maximum monthly PITI payment under the 28% housing ratio guideline?

A) $658.0

B) $1,692

C) $2,632

D) $6,768

41

Which of the following will happen to an apartment under a lease that becomes unusable due to smoke from a fire in an adjacent unit?

A) It is the landlord's responsibility to immediately terminate the lease

B) The requirement of the tenant is to remain in the apartment until it is condemned

C) It is termed an actual eviction

D) It is termed a constructive eviction

42

Which of the following refers to the increase in the principal balance of a loan due to making payments that fail to cover the interest due?

A) Deficiency

B) Negative amortization

C) Wrap around mortgage

D) Usury

CONTINUE ▶

43

Which of the following describes a recapture of depreciation?

A) The state government seizing property from an unpopular person

B) The federal government forcing elderly property owners into the street

C) The federal government recovering sheltered taxes after the sale of an investment property

D) A municipality fining property owners for unsatisfactory property maintenance

44

Which of the following refers to paying off a loan by making installment payments?

A) Amortization

B) Habendum

C) Satisfaction

D) Usury

45

A property initially purchased for $1,000,000 increased in value by 7% per year for three years.

Which of the following was the value of the property after the third year?

A) $1,230,000

B) $1,225,043

C) $1,210,000

D) $1,200,000

46

The **Fair Housing Act** bans the refusal to rent or sell a dwelling to any person because of race, color, religion, sex, familial status, or national origin.

Which of the following groups does the Federal Fair Housing Act of 1968 apply to?

A) Only people in the 15 southeastern states of the United States

B) Only those states that do not have state fair housing laws

C) Landlords and homeowners only

D) None of the above

A salesperson sold a property for $312,000. The salesperson's commission was 20% of the 6% commission paid by the owner.

After buying a gift for the new homeowners valued at $120, the salesperson will take home how much money?

A) $3,624
B) $3,744
C) $3,864
D) $3,920

In which of the following scenarios should the state mandated disclosure statement be presented to prospective clients?

A) When the transaction goes into contract
B) Only if the customer or client buys or sells a property through the broker
C) At the first substantive meeting
D) When there is a common understanding

SECTION 1

#	Answer	Topic	Subtopic	#	Answer	Topic	Subtopic	#	Answer	Topic	Subtopic	#	Answer	Topic	Subtopic
1	A	TB	SB1	13	C	TD	SD1	25	B	TD	SD1	37	C	TC	SC5
2	B	TA	SA3	14	B	TD	SD3	26	D	TA	SA5	38	D	TA	SA5
3	A	TC	SC3	15	D	TA	SA6	27	A	TD	SD1	39	D	TA	SA4
4	A	TC	SC5	16	C	TA	SA2	28	D	TC	SC2	40	C	TB	SB3
5	D	TC	SC2	17	A	TD	SD1	29	B	TD	SD3	41	D	TC	SC2
6	C	TA	SA4	18	C	TA	SA1	30	D	TA	SA3	42	B	TB	SB2
7	B	TB	SB4	19	A	TC	SC6	31	A	TB	SB2	43	C	TD	SD2
8	A	TB	SB4	20	D	TD	SD1	32	C	TC	SC3	44	A	TB	SB2
9	D	TD	SD2	21	B	TB	SB4	33	D	TA	SA3	45	B	TB	SB3
10	A	TA	SA5	22	B	TB	SB1	34	D	TC	SC3	46	D	TA	SA4
11	B	TC	SC3	23	B	TD	SD2	35	D	TC	SC2	47	A	TB	SB3
12	A	TC	SC2	24	B	TC	SC4	36	C	TA	SA1	48	C	TA	SA2

Topics & Subtopics

Code	Description	Code	Description
SA1	License Law	SC3	Construction & Environmental Issues
SA2	Law of Agency	SC4	Valuation
SA3	Land Use & Regulations	SC5	Property Management
SA4	Human Rights & Fair Housing	SC6	Real Estate Investment & Analysis
SA5	Municipal Agencies	SD1	Taxes Assessment
SA6	Condominiums & Suites	SD2	Income Tax Issues
SB1	Estates & Interests	SD3	Property Insurance
SB2	Real Estate Finance	TA	Rules & Regulations
SB3	Real Estate Math	TB	Economics
SB4	Mortgage Brokerage	TC	Transactions & Processes
SC2	The contract of sales and leases	TD	Taxes & Insurance

CONTINUE ▶

TEST DIRECTION

DIRECTIONS

Read the questions carefully and then choose the ONE best answer to each question.

Be sure to allocate your time carefully so you are able to complete the entire test within the testing session. You may go back and review your answers at any time.

You may use any available space in your test booklet for scratch work.

Questions in this booklet are not actual test questions but they are the samples for commonly asked questions.

This test aims to cover all topics which may appear on the actual test. However some topics may not be covered.

Studying this booklet will be preparing you for the actual test. It will not guarantee improving your test score but it will help you pass your exam on the first attempt.

Some useful tips for answering multiple choice questions;

- Start with the questions that you can easily answer.

- Underline the keywords in the question.

- Be sure to read all the choices given.

- Watch for keywords such as NOT, always, only, all, never, completely.

- Do not forget to answer every question.

1

Tax assessment determines the value, and sometimes, the use of a property to calculate a property tax.

Which of the following is filed by a property owner that wishes to challenge his or her tax assessment?

A) Grievance

B) Levy

C) Lis pendens

D) Tax Lien

2

A **mortgage broker** functions as a middleman who brokers mortgage loans to others on behalf of individuals or businesses

Which of the following should mortgage brokers disclose to loan applicants as a requirement?

A) Fees

B) Net worth

C) Amount of credit line

D) All of the above

3

A **gross lease** is a lease where the tenant pays a flat rental amount, and the landlord pays for all property charges regularly incurred by the ownership.

Which of the following is true about a gross lease?

A) It requires the tenant to pay taxes and insurance.

B) It only applies to commercial properties.

C) It is vile and repulsive.

D) None of the above

4

A landlord has the right to deny a tenant to rent his dwelling due to certain circumstances which the State Laws allow.

Which of the following will the State Laws allow a landlord to refuse to rent to a tenant?

A) People with dogs

B) Rock musician

C) Prison records

D) All of the above

5

A **first mortgage** is a type mortgage in a first lien position on the property that secures the mortgage. A first mortgage has the priority over all the other liens or claims on a particular property in the event of default.

Which of the following are the highest priority liens?

A) Tax liens
B) Mortgage liens
C) Commercial liens
D) None of the above

6

Real estate appraisal describes the process of creating an opinion of value for real property.

Which of the following is determined in a property first by a tax assessor like a real estate appraiser?

A) Assessed Value
B) Insured Value
C) Market Value
D) Mortgage Value

7

An **encumbrance** is a kind of regulation, liability, charge, or claim that is legally binding upon a property of an individual or entity. This may affect the clarity of a good title or may diminish the value of property, but may not prevent transfer of title.

Which of the following can be a form of encumberance?

A) Right of Way
B) Real estate tax lien
C) Shared driveway
D) All of the above

8

Which of the following refers to the process where there is an increase in real property by nature such as the buildup of silt?

A) Accretion
B) Addition
C) Erosion
D) Probate

9

Personal property coverage refers to the type of insurance that can help protect the items in your home.

In which of the following basis is personal property covered in homeowner policy?

A) Deductible cost
B) Depreciated
C) Lost clause
D) Replacement cost

10

An **assessed value** refers to the value assigned to a property to measure applicable taxes.

Which of the following determines the assessed value of a property?

A) Municipal council
B) Planning board
C) Tax Assessor
D) Tax Collector

11

A **short-term gain** refers to the capital gain by the sale or exchange of a capital asset which is held for less than or equal to one year or less.

Which of the following is a short-term capital gain tax?

A) The taxpayer's marginal income tax rate
B) As passive income
C) As portfolio income
D) Five percent

12

Section 1031, a section of the U.S. Internal Revenue Service Code, allows investors to defer capital gain taxes on any exchange of these kind of properties for business or investment purposes.

Which of the following is the term that describes the properties involved in a 1031 exchange?

A) Community-owned properties
B) Like-kind properties
C) Vacant properties
D) Transitional properties

CONTINUE ▶

13

For which of the following losses does liability insurance protect the insured?

A) Injuries and damage to people
B) Fire
C) Windstorm
D) All of the above

14

Which of the following is termed for a legal description written regarding angles and distances?

A) Lot and Block
B) Metes and Bounds
C) Plat of Lots
D) None of the above

15

Which of the following refers to the overhanging tree branches extending over a property line?

A) Lien
B) Easement
C) Encroachment
D) All of the above

16

A **minor** under the law refers to a person under a certain age that is usually the age of majority which is the shift from childhood to adulthood. Generally, depending upon your state law, the age of majority is at some point between **18** and 21. It also depends on jurisdiction and application.

Which of the following is a contract entered into by a minor?

A) Exculpatory
B) Void
C) Voidable
D) Valid

21

CONTINUE ▶

17

A **Building Permit** is a type of authorization that is required by a government or other regulatory body, and it must be granted before the construction of a new or existing building can legally occur.

Which of the following is the purpose of a building permit?

A) Ensuring that the sanitary conditions for septic systems are met

B) Ensuring that the community is developing in accordance with the master plan

C) Ensuring that the building facades are culturally correct

D) None of the above

18

A **percolation test** refers to a test that determines the water absorption rate of soil in preparation for the building of a septic drain field or infiltration basin.

Which of the following people administers the percolation test?

A) Department of Buildings

B) Department of Health

C) Building inspector

D) Tax assessor

19

Salary refers to a fixed compensation paid to a person for regular work or services.

Which of the following classifications do salaries fall in?

A) Active income

B) Non-active income

C) Passive income

D) Non-passive income

20

Federal Agencies are special government organizations which have been set up for specific purposes such as the management of different resources, financial oversight of industries or national security issues.

Which of the following is the federal agency concerned with environmental matters?

A) FHA

B) EPA

C) DEC

D) SOB

21

Which of the following refers to the situation called **Pro-ration** during a corporate action in which the available cash or shares are not sufficient to satisfy the offers tendered by shareholders?

A) The apportionment of expenses and assets of buyer and seller at closing

B) The time necessary for a variance to hold before the planning board

C) The process of a government taking an individual's land under eminent domain

D) The process of settling a will

22

What ownership form exists when a corporation owns real estate?

A) In severalty

B) Tenants in common

C) In trust

D) By the entirety

23

Which of the following refers to the act of giving a property to a municipal government for public use?

A) Regurgitation
B) Gestation
C) Grantation
D) Dedication

24

A **security deposit** refers to the deposit money to the landlord to assure the payment of rent and other responsibilities of the lease performed.

Which of the following would the security deposit the lessor has on hand for a tenant appear on in the closing statement?

A) Credit to the seller
B) Debit to the seller
C) Neither A nor B
D) Both A & B

25

Which of the following is determined when a real estate agent gathers data for a seller?

A) A reasonable asking price for the property on the market
B) The exact value of the property on that particular date
C) The value a lender will place on the property when it is purchased
D) None of the above

26

Real estates can be owned by different forms of ownership.

Which of the following about the ownership forms is not correct?

A) Unity of title means co-owners possess the same form of ownership.
B) Unity of time means co-owners receive title to real property at the same time and in the same deed.
C) Unity of interest means co-owners possess different percentage of ownership in the property.
D) Unity of possession means co-owners have equal access to all portions of the property.

CONTINUE ▶

27

A **life estate** refers to the land ownership for a person's lifetime in common and statutory law. However, in legal terms, it is an estate that will terminate at death in which a property can transfer to another person or revert to the original owner.

Which of the following is the interest in a life estate held by a grantor?

A) Reversionary Interest
B) Remainder Interest
C) Primary Interest
D) Interest rate

28

A **fixture** is a furniture or equipment in a fixed position.

Which of the following refers to the fixture used in the conduct of a business operating under a lease?

A) Chattel
B) Personal fixture
C) Primary interest
D) Trade fixture

29

The **vacancy rate** describes the percentage of empty units in a rental property which is available at a particular time.

What is the vacancy factor goal of an apartment building's property manager?

A) 3%
B) 10%
C) 95%
D) 100%

30

Insurance is a contract in which an individual or entity receives financial protection or reimbursement against losses from an insurance company.

Which of the following refers to an insurance policy that provides only one area of coverage?

A) Limited basis policy
B) Monoline policy
C) Package policy
D) Wide area indemnity policy

Tax deduction refers to a reduction of income which is taxed and commonly a result of expenses from those incurred to produce additional income.

For which of the following can a homeowner take an income tax deduction?

A) Paid mortgage interest

B) Real estate taxes

C) Paid student loan interest

D) All of the above

A **Real Estate License** is the authorization issued by state government, giving agents and brokers the ability to legally represent a home seller or buyer in the process of buying or selling real estate.

Which of the following individual is required to have a real estate license according to State Real Estate Laws?

A) Auctioneer

B) Executor

C) Practicing Attorney

D) None of the above

33

A parcel of property having an area of 2,760,000 square feet has a width of 2,400 feet.

How deep is the property?

A) 780 feet
B) 900 feet
C) 1,150 feet
D) 3,200 feet

34

The **Condominium Act** (Rights of the Unit Owners) requires the unit owners association, as well as its Board of Directors, to comply with the act, and with the condominium's declaration, bylaws, rules and regulations. This act requires that the bylaws specify the methods of selecting and removing board members and the board's powers and duties, including terms of office.

Which of the following about the bylaws of a condominium development is true?

A) It is only a formality to get municipal approvals for the development
B) They are the regulations by which the Association manages the development
C) It is not given to purchasers until binding contracts are signed
D) None of the above

35

Which of the following is a type of policy that covers an insured above and beyond standard policy limits?

A) All-inclusive
B) All-peril
C) Total-coverage
D) Umbrella

36

A person's **primary residence** refers to the dwelling place where he/she usually lives. It is typically a house or an apartment.

How much profit exemption does the IRS allow a single person selling a primary residence?

A) $1,000,000
B) $500,000
C) $250,000
D) $100,000

37

Tacking refers to a legal concept arising under a common law relating to competing priorities between two or more security interests arising over the same asset.

Which of the following defines the process of tacking?

A) Adding successive time periods for owners and former owners to acquire an easement

B) Establishing a lien on a property through a court action

C) Filing a lis pendens with the county clerk

D) None of the above

38

Which of the following describes the combination of two or more parcels of land into one track that has higher total value than the sum of individual plots?

A) Affirmative easement

B) Plottage

C) Plot planting

D) Undue influence

39

Which of the following is the rate for taxpayers if a taxpayer has a tax bracket of 28%?

A) 20%

B) 15%

C) 10%

D) 5%

40

A **mechanic's lien** refers to the security interest in property's title for the benefit of those who have supplied materials or labor that gives improvement to the property.

Which of the following places a mechanics lien on a property?

A) Administrator

B) Former owner

C) Home improvement contractor

D) Owner

41

Personal property generally refers to any asset other than real estate. The distinguishing factor between personal property and real estate is that personal property is movable; that is, the asset is not fixed permanently to one location as with real property, such as land or buildings.

Which of the following also refers to personal property?

A) Cattle

B) Chattel

C) Estate

D) Realty

42

A broker must subordinate his or her personal interests to which of the following personnel?

A) Client

B) Sales agent

C) Third party

D) Customer

43

Condominiums are classified as real state properties, meaning that buyers own the deeds to their dwellings. Buying into a co-op lets you become a shareholder in the corporation entitled of the property. As a shareholder, you are qualified for the exclusive use of a housing unit in the property.

Which of the following should a prospective co-op purchaser have to meet?

A) The city council

B) The broker's attorney

C) The Board of Directors

D) The building superintendent

44

Which of the following is the proper term for a tenant who defaults on a lease but remains in the premises?

A) Ingrate

B) Codicil

C) Tenant at sufferance

D) Tenant by the entirety

CONTINUE ▶

45

A commission of $13,200 was received by a broker for selling a property priced at $240,000.

What was the broker's commission rate?

A) 5.0%

B) 5.5%

C) 6.0%

D) 6.5%

46

In which of the following scenarios should the state mandated disclosure statement be presented to prospective clients?

A) When the transaction goes into contract

B) Only if the customer or client buys or sells a property through the broker

C) At the first substantive meeting

D) When there is a common understanding

47

Which of the following is the maximum lawful percentage rate a property manager may charge a property owner?

A) 10%

B) 7%

C) 5%

D) None of the above

48

Which of the following type of arrangements is useful when companies need to unbind the invested money in an asset for other investments, but the asset still needs to operate?

A) Contingency

B) Joint venture

C) Sale and leaseback

D) Secondary market

SECTION 2

#	Answer	Topic	Subtopic	#	Answer	Topic	Subtopic	#	Answer	Topic	Subtopic	#	Answer	Topic	Subtopic
1	A	TD	SD1	13	A	TD	SD3	25	A	TC	SC4	37	A	TB	SB1
2	A	TB	SB4	14	B	TC	SC1	26	C	TB	SB1	38	B	TC	SC4
3	D	TC	SC2	15	C	TB	SB1	27	A	TB	SB1	39	B	TD	SD2
4	D	TA	SA4	16	C	TC	SC2	28	D	TB	SB1	40	C	TB	SB1
5	A	TB	SB1	17	B	TA	SA5	29	D	TC	SC5	41	B	TB	SB1
6	C	TD	SD1	18	B	TA	SA5	30	B	TD	SD3	42	A	TA	SA2
7	D	TB	SB1	19	A	TD	SD2	31	D	TB	SB2	43	C	TA	SA6
8	A	TC	SC1	20	B	TC	SC3	32	A	TA	SA1	44	C	TC	SC2
9	D	TD	SD3	21	A	TC	SC1	33	C	TB	SB3	45	B	TB	SB3
10	C	TD	SD1	22	A	TB	SB1	34	B	TA	SA6	46	C	TA	SA2
11	A	TD	SD2	23	D	TC	SC1	35	D	TD	SD3	47	D	TC	SC5
12	B	TD	SD2	24	B	TC	SC1	36	C	TD	SD2	48	C	TB	SB2

Topics & Subtopics

Code	Description	Code	Description
SA1	License Law	SC3	Construction & Environmental Issues
SA2	Law of Agency	SC4	Valuation
SA4	Human Rights & Fair Housing	SC5	Property Management
SA5	Municipal Agencies	SD1	Taxes Assessment
SA6	Condominiums & Suites	SD2	Income Tax Issues
SB1	Estates & Interests	SD3	Property Insurance
SB2	Real Estate Finance	TA	Rules & Regulations
SB3	Real Estate Math	TB	Economics
SB4	Mortgage Brokerage	TC	Transactions & Processes
SC1	Deeds & Title Closing Costs	TD	Taxes & Insurance
SC2	The contract of sales and leases		

CONTINUE ▶

TEST DIRECTION

Read the questions carefully and then choose the ONE best answer to each question.

Be sure to allocate your time carefully so you are able to complete the entire test within the testing session. You may go back and review your answers at any time.

You may use any available space in your test booklet for scratch work.

Questions in this booklet are not actual test questions but they are the samples for commonly asked questions.

This test aims to cover all topics which may appear on the actual test. However some topics may not be covered.

Studying this booklet will be preparing you for the actual test. It will not guarantee improving your test score but it will help you pass your exam on the first attempt.

Some useful tips for answering multiple choice questions;

- Start with the questions that you can easily answer.

- Underline the keywords in the question.

- Be sure to read all the choices given.

- Watch for keywords such as NOT, always, only, all, never, completely.

- Do not forget to answer every question.

1

When you apply for a home loan, you can apply for a government-backed loan.

What type of loans are not insured or guaranteed by the US Government?

A) Conventional loans

B) FHA (Federal Housing Administration) loans

C) VA (Veterans Affairs) loans

D) All of the above

2

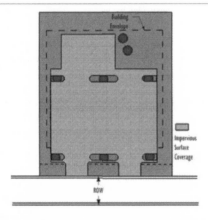

Setbacks refer to the imposed building restrictions on property owners. Local governments create setbacks through ordinances and Building Codes according to public policies such as safety, privacy, and environmental protection.

Which of the following refers to the setback?

A) Judgment

B) Disappointment

C) Sheathing

D) Mandated distance

3

Good Faith Estimate refers to an estimate of fees that is due at closing for a mortgage loan which must be provided by a lender to a borrower.

Which of the following is the number of business days during which a loan applicant must receive a good faith estimate?

A) Thirty

B) Ten

C) Seven

D) Three

4

How do unused prepaid taxes appear on a closing statement?

A) As a credit to the seller

B) As a credit to the buyer

C) Both A and B

D) Neither A nor B

5

The **trustee** manages or holds assets, cash or a property title.

Which of the following benefits when the trustee held in a property?

A) Beneficiary
B) Decedent
C) Grantor
D) Heir

6

An **automatic renewal clause** also called as self-renewal or evergreen clause acts to renew a contract if notice to terminate perpetually is not provided within a generally specific and relatively small window of time (for example, 30 days before the end of the term).

Which of the following refers to an automatic renewal clause in a lease?

A) It is illegal
B) It is good for the tenant
C) It is good for the landlord
D) It is good for both the landlord and the tenant

7

Lally Column is a tubular steel column filled with concrete. It is used as a supporting member in a building.

Where are these normally found?

A) Closets
B) Bathrooms
C) Basement
D) Attic

8

Property valuation refers to the process of developing an opinion of value for real property.

Which of the following is correct regarding the effects of income and expenses on the valuation of a property?

A) Lower profit means higher property value
B) The profit has no relation to property value
C) Higher profit means higher property value
D) Profit has no effect on the property value.

9

Which of the following refers to an executed contract?

A) It is fully completed

B) It is not yet fully completed

C) It is fully signed

D) It is not yet fully signed

10

Which of the following document is issued when an improvement is made to a property and the building inspector passes it?

A) Building permit

B) Certificate of Occupancy

C) Tax assessment

D) Deed

11

If a real estate agent suggests to a client to move to a particular area to reside in a community which he can fit, he can be guilty for which of the following?

A) Steering

B) Bockbusting

C) Flipping

D) Redlining

12

The **interest and principal payment** on a mortgage is the main component of a monthly mortgage payment. The principal payment refers to the amount borrowed and had to get paid back, and interest refers to the charges that lenders set for the lending money.

Which of the following constitutes mortgage interest and principal payments?

A) Debt service

B) Cash flow

C) Vacancy factor

D) Variable expenses

13

Earnest money refers to a deposit made to a seller showing the buyer's good faith in a transaction.

Which of the following does an earnest money deposit appear on in a closing statement?

A) Credit to buyer
B) Credit to seller
C) Debit to buyer
D) Debit to seller

14

Which of the following is true about the desired profit that an investor uses to determine the value of a property?

A) Every investor has a personal choice for his/her desired profit.
B) Increasing expenses results in the desired profit.
C) The desired profit does not affect property valuation.
D) Every month, the desired profit is one percent of the purchase price.

15

Which of the following can a licensee share his or her earned commission with?

A) Seller
B) Customer
C) Postal worker providing a lead
D) No one

16

All building tenants use meeting spaces, lobbies, restrooms and other amenities in which landlords also charge for the use of these spaces.

Which of the following is the basis of an office building tenant in paying rent?

A) Carpetable square feet
B) Viable square feet
C) Usable square feet
D) Rentable square feet

17

Tax assessment determines the value, and sometimes, the use of a property to calculate a property tax.

Which of the following is the first step in contesting a property's tax assessment?

A) To meet with the mayor
B) To meet with the building inspector
C) To meet with the tax assessor
D) To meet with the tax collector

18

British Thermal Unit (BTU) is part of the British Imperial system of units, its counterpart in the metric system.

Which of the following does the British Thermal Unit measure?

A) Energy
B) Electricity
C) Skill
D) Temperature

19

Net operating income or NOI refers to a calculation used to analyze real estate investment generating income.

To determine net operating income, from which of the following are the expenses deducted from?

A) Vacancy factor
B) Cash flow
C) Gross income
D) Variable income

20

Which of the following refers to an appraisal process which uses comparisons of similar properties in the same neighborhood?

A) Cost Approach
B) Market Data Approach
C) Pricing Method
D) All of the above

21

Which of the following given items below is not a necessary element of a contract?

A) Consideration
B) Competent parties
C) Earnest money
D) Meeting of the minds

22

A **sales agent** is an authorized individual by a corporation or manufacturer that sells or distributes his products within a given territory.

Which of the following usually applies to a sales agent?

A) Volunteer
B) Employee
C) Independent contractor
D) None of the above

23

Market value should exchange on the date of valuation between a willing buyer and a willing seller in an arms-length transaction after proper marketing wherein the parties had each acted knowledgeably, prudently.

Which of the following refers to the factor that exerts the least amount of influence on the value of a seller's property?

A) Local economy

B) Location

C) Supply and demand

D) The listing agent's opinion

24

An **elected official** refers to a person who is an official by an election. Which of the following are not elected?

A) City Council members

B) Board of Trustee members

C) Town Council members

D) Planning Board members

25

Comparables (also know as comps) is a real estate appraisal term that refers to different properties with similar characteristics to a subject property whose value is being sought.

Which of the following is the minimum of comps required mostly by secondary lenders to ensure an accurate estimation of a value when performing the sales comparison approach?

A) 2

B) 3

C) 4

D) 5

26

An **independent contractor** is an individual, business, or corporation that provides goods or services to another entity under terms specified in a contract.

In which of the following scenarios will the Federal Government accept a sales agent as an independent contractor?

A) The agent is paid strictly on a commission basis

B) The agent works out of his or her own home

C) The agent earns no money

D) The agent has another job

27

Which of the following can be the best description of a property's market value?

A) Listing price

B) Most recent selling price

C) Most probable selling price

D) Appraised value for property tax purposes

28

Which of the following is a contract that binds only one party?

A) Unilateral contract

B) Bilateral contract

C) Binder

D) Implied contract

29

A **joint tenancy** is an ownership wherein each co-tenant owns an undivided share of the property just as in a tenancy in common. Four conditions are required for the formation of joint tenancy. Three of them are time, title and possession.

Which of the following is the fourth condition?

A) Incontinence

B) Interest

C) Loyalty

D) Trust

30

John is working as a municipal tax assessor. Which of the following is John's role?

A) He sets the tax collector's goals

B) He determines the value of properties in the community

C) He determines the tax rate property owners pay

D) He collects taxes from property owners

31

A broker can practice depositing trust funds into the firm's operating account.

Which of the following best describes this situation if the broker acts upon it?

A) Commingling

B) Diversion

C) Mingling

D) Misappropriating

32

Dual agency is a situation in which a real estate agent works with both the buyer and the seller.

Which of the following scenario best describes Dual Agency?

A) A real estate broker operating two real estate offices

B) A method whereby two sales agents split a commission on a transaction

C) It is illegal if both parties don't have knowledge and consent

D) A combination of real estate and insurance being offered at the same time

33

Economic obsolescence refers to a form of depreciation due to unfavorable external conditions to the property such as the local economy, encroachment of objectionable enterprises, and other factors.

Which of the following describes an example of economic obsolescence?

A) A ruined roof

B) A junkyard down the block

C) An outmoded heating system

D) None of the above

34

Which of the following determines rents where rent control or rent stabilization is not in effect?

A) Board of Local Realtors

B) Current Market conditions

C) MLS; Multiple Listing Services

D) Regulations of municipalities

35

When a homeowner has a contract with an agent in selling a home, the listing agreement has a set expiration date.

Which of the following refers to the most common reason for listings expiring?

A) The property did not get adequate exposure to the market.

B) The property was not in a good location.

C) The property was in poor condition.

D) The property was priced too high.

36

Front foot is a standard measurement of land, applied at the frontage of its street line. It is used for lots of generally uniform depth in downtown areas.

A property with dimensions of 125 foot frontage and 250 foot depth was sold for $1,750,000. What was the price of the property per front foot?

A) $70.00

B) $1,400.00

C) $8,750.00

D) $14,000.00

37

A **land patent** is an exclusive land grant made by a sovereign entity with respect to a particular tract of land.

Which of the following is the use of a land patent?

A) To convey a public land to an individual

B) To fasten two parallel plates at a corner

C) To fasten two different plates at a corner

D) To correct an irregularity in a zoning law

38

A **Condemnation Suit** is a type of judicial proceeding filed against a property owner.

Which of the following is the condition when a Condemnation Suit is filed against a property owner?

A) Incentive zoning

B) Escheat

C) Eminent Domain

D) Variance

39

The **binding contract** refers to an agreement in writing between two or more individuals. If one negates to his/her promise as outlined in the contract, a court can impose penalties in the event.

Which of the following must be given to a person before signing a binding contract to purchase a condominium?

A) A bond

B) A survey

C) A blank contract

D) A Public Offering Statement

40

Remainderman refers to a person who inherits or is entitled to inherit property upon the termination of the estate of the former owner.

Which of the following also refers to a remainderman?

A) Possesses a reversionary interest in real estate
B) The last one to leave
C) Holds over at the termination of a lease
D) Receives real estate upon the demise of a life tenant

41

Which of the following is the rate of return of a building earning $80,000 annually that had a purchase price of $750,000?

A) 9.4%
B) 12%
C) 15%
D) 10.6%

42

Licensee refers to a person or business that holds an approved license to conduct an activity, such as operating a business.

Which of the following must a licensee do when she is selling her property?

A) The property should be listed with the MLS
B) The licensee must disclose the fact that he or she is a licensed real estate agent to prospective buyers
C) The property must be listed at fair market value
D) All of the above

43

A **broker** is a person or individual who buys and sells goods or assets for others.

Which of the following choices refers to the practice of brokers profiting by creating panic selling in a neighborhood?

A) Redlining
B) Blockbusting
C) Soliciting
D) Steering

44

Which of the following documents creates a relationship between a property owner and a broker?

A) Operating Statement

B) Management Agreement

C) Rent Roll

D) State Property Manager License

45

Usury became common first in England under the rule of King Henry VIII.

Which of the following most accurately describes usury?

A) Charging an illegally high-interest rate for borrowed funds

B) To charge fees for borrowing money

C) It is the illegal use of another's money

D) It is the illegal use of another's property

46

Housing discrimination is a type of discrimination wherein an individual or a family that tries to buy, rent, lease, sell or finance a home is treated unequally based on certain characteristics, like race, class, sex, religion, national origin, and familial status.

Which of the following is needed to prove that the complainant experienced an incident of discrimination?

A) The act was in a pattern of discrimination

B) The act caused a loss

C) The act was intentional

D) Discrimination occurred

47

A property which was purchased one year ago for $1,750,000 is now valued at $1,915,000. What is the percentage rate of appreciation?

A) 8.6%

B) 9.4%

C) 18.9%

D) 84.0%

An investor requires a 15.5% rate of return. A listed property priced at $1,550,000 has a monthly income of $72,340 and monthly expenses of $52,760.

Does the property meet the investor's requirement? What should the offering price be to meet the demand?

A) No. $1,515,870.90
B) No. $1,483,671.15
C) No. $1,478,765.30
D) Yes.

SECTION 3

#	Answer	Topic	Subtopic	#	Answer	Topic	Subtopic	#	Answer	Topic	Subtopic	#	Answer	Topic	Subtopic
1	A	TB	SB2	13	A	TC	SC1	25	B	TB	SB4	37	A	TC	SC1
2	D	TA	SA3	14	A	TB	SB6	26	A	TA	SA2	38	C	TA	SA3
3	D	TC	SC1	15	D	TA	SA1	27	C	TB	SB5	39	D	TA	SA6
4	B	TC	SC1	16	D	TB	SB5	28	A	TC	SC2	40	D	TB	SB1
5	A	TB	SB1	17	C	TA	SA5	29	B	TB	SB1	41	D	TB	SB5
6	A	TC	SC2	18	A	TC	SC3	30	B	TA	SA5	42	B	TA	SA1
7	C	TC	SC3	19	C	TB	SB5	31	A	TA	SA1	43	B	TA	SA4
8	D	TB	SB6	20	B	TC	SC4	32	C	TA	SA2	44	B	TC	SC5
9	A	TC	SC2	21	C	TC	SC2	33	B	TC	SC4	45	A	TB	SB2
10	B	TA	SA3	22	C	TA	SA2	34	B	TC	SC5	46	D	TA	SA4
11	A	TC	SC6	23	D	TC	SC4	35	D	TC	SC4	47	B	TB	SB3
12	A	TB	SB5	24	D	TA	SA4	36	D	TB	SB3	48	A	TB	SB3

Topics & Subtopics

Code	Description	Code	Description
SA1	License Law	SB6	Income Approach to Real Estate Valuation
SA2	Law of Agency	SC1	Deeds & Title Closing Costs
SA3	Land Use & Regulations	SC2	The contract of sales and leases
SA4	Human Rights & Fair Housing	SC3	Construction & Environmental Issues
SA5	Municipal Agencies	SC4	Valuation
SA6	Condominiums & Suites	SC5	Property Management
SB1	Estates & Interests	SC6	Real Estate Investment & Analysis
SB2	Real Estate Finance	TA	Rules & Regulations
SB3	Real Estate Math	TB	Economics
SB4	Mortgage Brokerage	TC	Transactions & Processes
SB5	Commercial Investment		

CONTINUE ▶

TEST DIRECTION

Read the questions carefully and then choose the ONE best answer to each question.

Be sure to allocate your time carefully so you are able to complete the entire test within the testing session. You may go back and review your answers at any time.

You may use any available space in your test booklet for scratch work.

Questions in this booklet are not actual test questions but they are the samples for commonly asked questions.

This test aims to cover all topics which may appear on the actual test. However some topics may not be covered.

Studying this booklet will be preparing you for the actual test. It will not guarantee improving your test score but it will help you pass your exam on the first attempt.

Some useful tips for answering multiple choice questions;

- Start with the questions that you can easily answer.

- Underline the keywords in the question.

- Be sure to read all the choices given.

- Watch for keywords such as NOT, always, only, all, never, completely.

- Do not forget to answer every question.

1

Conservative investing is a type of investment strategy that seeks to preserve an investment portfolio's value by investing in lower risk securities. Conservative investors have their risk tolerance range from low to moderate. Some good examples of conservative investing strategies are capital preservation and current income.

Which of the following should a conservative investor consider in order to conserve a capital?

A) Industrial parks
B) Regional shopping malls
C) Highly leveraged properties
D) Fee simple purchases

2

Which of the following offers the greatest assurance of title?

A) Bargain and Sale deed
B) Quitclaim deed
C) Sheriff's deed
D) Warranty deed

3

A **capital improvement** refers to the addition of a permanent structural change or the restoration of a property that will either enhance the property's overall value or increase its useful life or adapt it to a new use.

What cost is considered to be a capital improvement rather than an expense?

A) Roof repair
B) Salesperson commission
C) Addition of a two-car garage
D) A for-sale sign on the property

4

Which of the following describes the part of a lease that states the intention of the lessor and the lessee?

A) Passage clause
B) Usage clause
C) Demising clause
D) Allowance clause

5

A **stand-alone house** also called a single-detached residence, is a free-standing residential building. It is sometimes referred to as a single family home as opposed to a multi-family residential dwelling.

Which of the following is the appraisal approach commonly used in appraising single-family housing?

A) Rental approach

B) Income approach

C) Cost approach

D) Sales comparison approach

6

Cooperative housing is another type of home ownership. Instead of owning an actual real estate with cooperative housing, you own a part of a corporation that owns the building. Cooperative housing usually includes an apartment building or buildings.

Which type of income is not considered on a loan application for a cooperative unit purchase?

A) Gambling

B) Commissions

C) Barter income

D) Alimony

7

An **agent** is a seller acting upon the authority of an owner while the client is the one that is buying goods or properties through the agent.

Which of the following best describes the act of an agent following lawful instructions of a client?

A) Accounting

B) Obedience

C) Care

D) Loyalty

8

For which of the following expenses an investment property seller must be able to give accurate figures?

A) Property taxes

B) Finance costs

C) Insurance

D) All of the above

CONTINUE ▶

9

Homeowner's insurance refers to a type of property insurance which covers losses and damages to an individual's house and assets in the home.

Which of the following is not covered by a standard coverage homeowner policy?

A) Fire

B) Flood

C) Theft

D) Vandalism

10

Collateral is a property or asset that a borrower offers as a way for a lender to secure the loan.

Which of the following collaterals is needed for a co-op purchaser to purchase a loan?

A) A co-op building stock

B) A property deed

C) Title policy

D) A bond

11

Which of the following choices describes the legal method of decreasing an investor's taxable income?

A) Return on investment

B) Insurance claim

C) Tax shelter

D) Vacancy loss

12

Capital gain refers to the value increase of a real estate resulting in a higher worth than the purchase price.

How long must an asset be held to be a long-term capital gain?

A) More than five years

B) More than one year

C) More than six months

D) More than three months

13

A **life estate** refers to the land ownership for a person's lifetime in common and statutory law. However, in legal terms, it is an estate that will terminate at death in which a property can transfer to another person or revert to the original owner.

For which of the following can life estate be created?

A) Any person
B) Only a trustee
C) Only a relative
D) None of the above

14

An **agency** is a business or institution built to provide different or specific services which typically involves organizing transactions between two parties.

Which of the following can be represented by an agent in a single agency?

A) Buyer
B) Seller
C) Either the seller or the buyer
D) Both seller and buyer

15

Which of the following is not one of the functions of the Real Estate Settlement Procedures Act (RESPA)?

A) Mandating certain disclosures in connection with the real estate settlement process
B) Prohibiting certain unlawful practices by real estate settlement providers, such as kickbacks
C) Informing borrowers about all mortgage options
D) Helping home purchasers make informed decisions regarding their real estate transactions

16

Mortgage refers to a loan which is secured by real estate or property. In exchange for funds received by the homebuyer to buy property or a home, a lender gets the promise of that buyer to pay back the funds within a specific time frame for a particular cost.

Which of the following makes home mortgages available to the public?

A) Savings banks
B) Mortgage bankers
C) Credit unions
D) All of the above

17

Deed refers to a legal document which is an official record and proof of ownership of property.

Which of the following is a must for deeds to be recorded?

A) It should be written
B) It should be acknowledged
C) Both A and B
D) Neither A nor B

18

In the United States, a **historic district** is a group of buildings, properties, or sites that have been designated by one of several entities on different levels as historically or architecturally significant.

Which of the following areas of a historic district requires permission to alter?

A) Plumbing fixtures
B) Dining areas
C) The exterior of a building
D) The interior of a building

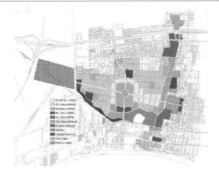

## 19

Zoning is a legal mechanism for local governments to regulate the use of privately owned real properties. Through community planning and development, zoning laws help local governmental agencies preserve property values and ensure that communities are functional and safe places.

Which of the following is not affected by Zoning?

A) The distance a structure may be erected from a property line

B) The number of parking spaces for a fast food restaurant

C) The interior of a building

D) Private property

A **multiple listing service** (MLS) is a type of service used by a group of real estate brokers where they band together to create an MLS that allows each one of them to see one another's listings of properties for sale.

Which of the following should be immediately called by the licensee upon obtaining a written offer on an MLS property?

A) The property owner

B) The listing broker

C) MLS

D) None of the above

21

Property insurance provides reimbursement to the owner or tenant of a property in the event of damage or theft.

Which of the following has the most influence on a property's insurance cost?

A) Paid fire department
B) Property value
C) State Laws
D) Town Council

22

A mortgage broker is a middleman that is working with a borrower and a lender while qualifying the borrower for a mortgage.

The broker gathers income, asset and employment documentations, a credit report and other information for assessing the borrower's ability to secure financing.

Which of the following can compensate a mortgage broker?

A) The lender
B) The borrower
C) Neither A nor B
D) Both A and B

23

A **Public Offering Statement (POS)** is a type of document provided by the builder to the buyers of a condominium. It contains the details about condominium's structure and management, including its CC&Rs. It also contains important disclosures about budgets, insurance, construction and rules for the condo.

For it to be reviewed, a Public Offering Statement must be submitted to which of the following?

A) Department of Health
B) Department of Banking
C) Department of State
D) State Attorney General

24

A **printed circuit board** (PCB) is to support and connect electronic parts using conductive pads, tracks and other properties etched from copper sheets laminated onto a non-conductive substrate.

Which of the following have PCBs?

A) Aerosol cans
B) Air Condition Systems
C) Electrical equipment
D) Heating Units

To be licensed, a Salesperson must be at least 18 years old with no felony or misdemeanor. She must be a permanent resident of the United States and must have accomplished the course, passed the State Exam, and have paid the license fee.

A person completed the course and passed the school examination but she has not taken the state examination yet. Which of the following can this person do?

A) Explain the advantages of the house to prospective buyers

B) Discuss pricing strategies with prospective sellers

C) Show houses listed on the MLS to prospective buyers

D) Start collecting information about the community and the neighborhood where she will work

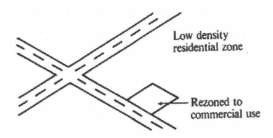

Which of the following best describes the use of Spot Zoning?

A) Used primarily to bring new businesses to an area

B) Used to bring property values in line with neighboring parcels of property

C) A use for land that serves a useful purpose to neighborhood residents

D) Used to control the number of people living in a zone

27

Which of the following describes a non-conforming use?

A) It is not legal

B) If the owner changes, it must be removed or closed

C) It does not confirm to the current local zoning laws, but it is permitted because it existed before

D) None of the above

28

You are trying to price a property which was sold for $1,450,000 fifteen years ago. The property values in this neighborhood have diminished by an average of 5% since then.

Which of the following is the estimated value of the property?

A) $825,000

B) $1,300,000

C) $1,377,500

D) $1,400,000

29

A **title** refers to proof of ownership on a property.

In which of the following is the least assurance of title offered?

A) A Trust deed

B) A Full Warranty Deed

C) A Bargain and Sale deed with covenants

D) A Bargain and Sale deed without covenants

30

The **right of survivorship** is a feature on some types of joint ownership of property, most notably joint tenancy and tenancy in common. When jointly owned property includes a right of survivorship, the surviving owner automatically absorbs a dying owner's share of the property.

To which of the following does the right of survivorship apply?

A) Holdover tenants

B) Tenants in common

C) Life tenants

D) Joint tenants

31

An **exclusive right to sell agreement** is a type of agreement that restricts the seller to list the property with any other agent in which the agent must be paid commission in certain circumstances.

In which of the following scenarios does commission not have to be paid?

A) When the property is not sold
B) When the property is sold by the seller
C) When the property is sold by a cooperating broker
D) When the property is sold by an uncooperative broker

32

Which of the following about the property does a purchaser need to prove to a lender to obtain a mortgage loan?

A) Property is deductible
B) Property is fireproof
C) Property is insured
D) Properly insulated

33

A 5-acre parcel of land was sold for $1,750,000. What was the price per square foot? (1 acre = 43,560 square feet)

A) $8.035
B) $40.175
C) $80.350
D) $35,000

34

Asbestos contains any of the several minerals (such as chrysotile) that readily separates into long flexible fibers, that cause asbestosis which have been implicated as causes of certain cancers. For many years it has been used as a fireproof insulating material in the buildings.

Which of the following can only remove asbestos?

A) General Contractor

B) The homeowner acting alone

C) Licensed asbestos remover companies

D) Licensed and bonded cleaning business

35

Cease and Desist Letter is a type of letter which advises a person to stop using specified legal rights which are claimed by another. A Cease and Desist Letter, signed and dated, demands an individual or a corporate entity to cease certain actions as they do not have a right to act accordingly.

Which of the following is The Cease and Desist Letter used for?

A) Protecting residents from unwanted solicitation

B) Determining ethnic demographics in various communities

C) Determining where brokers may obtain exclusive listings

D) None of the above

CONTINUE ▶

36

Urea-formaldehyde foam insulation (UFFI) was used extensively in the 1970s. Homeowners used UFFI as a wall cavity filler at the time to conserve energy. Then, it was injected inside the walls and the final product acted as an insulating agent.

Which of the following is the advantage of urea formaldehyde foam insulation over other insulations?

A) It is contaminant-free
B) It is easy to install
C) It is less expensive
D) None of the above

37

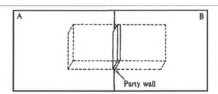

A **party wall** is a wall that is common in two adjoining rooms.

A party wall is an example of which of the following?

A) Easement
B) Incoherent
C) Encroachment
D) Appurtenance

38

According to which of the following does the remaining fuel in a storage tank at closing is being apportioned and paid?

A) The average price of the time the seller purchased it
B) The purchase price of the seller
C) Current market value
D) None of the above

39

A **quitclaim deed** refers to an instrument used in transferring interest in real property.

Which of the following is the use of quitclaim deed?

A) To remove a cloud on the title
B) To restore mining rights
C) To foreclose on a property by a lender
D) To transfer property from an estate to a heir

CONTINUE ▶

40

Market value should exchange on the date of valuation between a willing buyer and a willing seller in an arms-length transaction after proper marketing wherein the parties had each acted knowledgeably and prudently.

Which of the following percentages of market value must be insured for replacement cost to be in effect?

A) 20%

B) 25%

C) 75%

D) 80%

41

On a closing statement dated May 15th, how would a $1,600/month tenant's prepaid rent appear?

A) Debit buyer $800, Credit seller $800

B) Debit seller $800, Credit buyer $800

C) Debit buyer $800

D) Debit seller $800

42

A **certificate of occupancy** refers to a document issued by a local government agency to certify a building's compliance with applicable building codes and other laws. It indicates that the building is in a condition suitable for occupancy.

When can a Certificate of Occupancy can be issued?

A) After the tax assessor determines the value of the home improvement

B) After a construction job passes the final inspection of the building inspector

C) After a home improvement application is submitted to the building inspector

D) Only after approved plans are submitted

43

A **rate of return** refers to the loss or gain on an investment over a specified period of time in the percentage of the investment's cost.

An investment property's monthly net income is $14,240, and its monthly operating expenses are $8,120. If the investor paid $680,400 for the property, which of the following is the investor's rate of return?

A) 3.2%

B) 10.8%

C) 11.9%

D) 20.9%

44

When Aries bought his property he had a 20% down payment and secured a 30 year loan at 7% interest.

Which of the following is the amount he paid for the property if his first month's payment was $2,240.00?

A) $260,000

B) $290,000

C) $422,000

D) $480,000

CONTINUE ▶

SECTION 4

#	Answer	Topic	Subtopic	#	Answer	Topic	Subtopic	#	Answer	Topic	Subtopic	#	Answer	Topic	Subtopic
1	A	TB	SB5	12	B	TD	SD2	23	A	TA	SA6	34	C	TC	SC3
2	D	TC	SC1	13	A	TB	SB1	24	C	TC	SC3	35	C	TA	SA4
3	C	TD	SD2	14	B	TA	SA2	25	D	TA	SA1	36	D	TC	SC3
4	C	TC	SC2	15	C	TA	SA3	26	C	TA	SA3	37	A	TB	SB1
5	D	TB	SB4	16	D	TB	SB2	27	C	TA	SA3	38	C	TC	SC1
6	A	TA	SA6	17	C	TC	SC1	28	C	TB	SB1	39	A	TC	SC1
7	B	TA	SA2	18	C	TA	SA5	29	A	TC	SC1	40	D	TD	SD3
8	A	TC	SC6	19	C	TA	SA3	30	D	TB	SB1	41	B	TC	SC1
9	B	TD	SD3	20	B	TA	SA1	31	A	TA	SA2	42	B	TA	SA5
10	A	TA	SA6	21	B	TD	SD3	32	C	TD	SD3	43	B	TB	SB5
11	C	TB	SB5	22	D	TB	SB4	33	A	TB	SB3	44	C	TB	SB1

Topics & Subtopics

Code	Description	Code	Description
SA1	License Law	SC1	Deeds & Title Closing Costs
SA2	Law of Agency	SC2	The contract of sales and leases
SA3	Land Use & Regulations	SC3	Construction & Environmental Issues
SA4	Human Rights & Fair Housing	SC6	Real Estate Investment & Analysis
SA5	Municipal Agencies	SD2	Income Tax Issues
SA6	Condominiums & Suites	SD3	Property Insurance
SB1	Estates & Interests	TA	Rules & Regulations
SB2	Real Estate Finance	TB	Economics
SB3	Real Estate Math	TC	Transactions & Processes
SB4	Mortgage Brokerage	TD	Taxes & Insurance
SB5	Commercial Investment		

CONTINUE ▶

TEST DIRECTION

Read the questions carefully and then choose the ONE best answer to each question.

Be sure to allocate your time carefully so you are able to complete the entire test within the testing session. You may go back and review your answers at any time.

You may use any available space in your test booklet for scratch work.

Questions in this booklet are not actual test questions but they are the samples for commonly asked questions.

This test aims to cover all topics which may appear on the actual test. However some topics may not be covered.

Studying this booklet will be preparing you for the actual test. It will not guarantee improving your test score but it will help you pass your exam on the first attempt.

Some useful tips for answering multiple choice questions;

- Start with the questions that you can easily answer.

- Underline the keywords in the question.

- Be sure to read all the choices given.

- Watch for keywords such as NOT, always, only, all, never, completely.

- Do not forget to answer every question.

1

"Jurisdiction in rem" describes the exercise of power by a court over property or a "status" against a person over whom the court does not have in personam jurisdiction.

An in-rem procedure is against which of the following?

A) Municipal government

B) Property

C) Property owner

D) Retail business owner

2

A **landlord** is an individual who rents a land, a building, or an apartment to a tenant.

Which of the following should not be the basis where the landlord refuses a tenant?

A) Number of children in the family

B) Prison record of the tenants

C) Political affiliation of the tenants

D) All of the above

3

A **condominium** or a **condo** is a type of real estate property which is divided into several units that are separately owned and surrounded by common areas jointly owned.

Which of the following involves a condominium purchase?

A) Deed transfer

B) Purchase of corporate stock

C) Proprietary lease

D) Meeting with a Board of Directors

4

Which of the following happens for a taxpayer if losses exceed the allowable limit for that year?

A) The taxpayer will be penalized about 10% for the over the limit amount.

B) The lost passive is gone which can only be used in the specified tax year.

C) The loss may be carried over to a future year when the taxpayer meets passive activity limit loss rules.

D) The allowable limit goes up the same amount the following year.

5

Which of the following business structures generally does not require registration with the state?

A) C Corp

B) S Corp

C) LLC

D) General Partnership

6

A **contract clause** refers to a specific section within a written contract which defines the duties, rights, and privileges that each party has under the contract terms.

Which of the following describes a contract clause that will allow either party to void the contract if a certain condition occurs?

A) Cogency

B) Contingency

C) Deficiency

D) Disciple

7

Lien refers to the official order allowing someone to keep a person's property who owes them money until there is full payment.

Which of the following determines the priority of a lien?

A) Date of paying off the lien

B) Date of making the lien

C) Date of the court hearing

D) Date of recording the lien

8

Security means any written, electronic or oral agreement. It is secured by any lien or charge upon the capital, assets, profits, property or credit of any person or any public or governmental body, subdivision, or agency.

Which of the following refers to security in a real state?

A) Real Estate Investment Trust shares

B) An apartment building owned in a partnership

C) Both A and B

D) Neither A nor B

9

Which of the following does the IRS use to define a real estate professional?

A) The number of experience years in the real estate industry

B) The number of real estate properties owned

C) The number of hours worked in real estate each year

D) When the taxpayer is a licensed real estate agent or not

10

Source of income refers to where your money is coming from. An individual income can be from multiple sources such as employment, investment and welfare. On the other hand, business income can be from particular markets, products, customers, investments or government grants.

Which of the following is a source of income other than rent?

A) Vacancy

B) Laundromats

C) Property taxes

D) Mortgage interest

11

Which of the following does a loan originator use to determine the estimated value of a property based on an analytical comparison of similar property sales?

A) An appraisal

B) An area survey

C) A cost-benefit analysis

D) A market survey

12

Which of the following describes a tenancy by the entirety?

A) Ownership that is available only to married couples, tenancy by the entirety means that property may not be sold without the agreement of both parties.

B) Ownership which requires the four unities: Interest, Possession, Time, and Title

C) Ownership that is available for Limited Liabilities

D) Equal or unequal undivided ownership between two or more people

CONTINUE ▶

13

Section 1031 is under the section of the U.S. Internal Revenue Service Code tackling any exchange of properties for business or investment purposes.

Which of the following is the primary purpose of a 1031 exchange?

A) Transfer owned property to a family member before the owner's death without paying taxes.

B) Delay paying taxes when selling one rental investment and using the funds to purchase a similar income producing property.

C) Transfer the property to a non-family member upon the owner's death.

D) None of these answers are correct.

14

An **operating expense** refers to the ongoing cost for running a business, system or product.

Which of the following expenses are not included in calculating net operating expenses?

A) Mortgage Interest
B) Utility Charges
C) Property Insurance
D) Property Taxes

15

A **real estate investment trust** (REIT) means that a company operates or finances income-producing real estate.

Which of the following describes the process of taxing REIT dividends?

A) Investors pay taxes on dividends at their income tax rate.
B) Investors will pay taxes on dividends at the maximum federal income tax rate.
C) Dividends tax at capital gains rates.
D) REIT dividends tax at corporate income tax rates.

16

Fiduciary duties of a real estate agent refer to the broker or agent functions under specific legally mandated duties for a seller or buyer client interests or transactions.

Which of the following categories is under Fiduciary Duties of a Real Estate Agent?

A) Confidentiality
B) Accounting
C) Obedience
D) All of the above

17

There is a scam that entails homeowners who are encouraged to refinance their property over and over until little or no equity remains.

Which of the following is this type of scam called?

A) Loan flipping
B) Reverse equity
C) Extreme lending
D) Property skimming

18

A **Good Faith Estimate** (also called GFE) is a standard form that is required to be provided by a mortgage lender or broker to a consumer as mandated by the Federal Law.

Which of the following federal law requires the lender or broker to provide the GFE to the lendee within three business days of the date a loan application is taken?

A) RESPA
B) TILA
C) ECOA
D) HMDA

19

Which of the following is required to qualify as a limited partnership?

A) At least two general partners
B) At least two general partners and registration with the state
C) Two or more limited partners and an annual franchise fee paid to the state
D) At least one general partner and one limited partner

20

When someone dies having made a valid will, he or she dies "testate." Otherwise, he or she has died "intestate."

A person died "testate," but after an extensive search, there were no additional heirs found.

By which of the following ways should the person's real property be transferred?

A) Devise
B) Demise
C) Escheat to the estate
D) Descent and distribution

21

You referred a client to a lender. In return they sent you a thank-you note with a $100 gift card to a local restaurant.

Which of the following law makes this kickback illegal?

A) CRA
B) ECOA
C) Regulation Z
D) RESPA

22

Which of the following are some sources of revenue for calculating the net operating income?

A) Vending machine profits
B) Parking fees
C) Rent payments
D) All of these are correct answers

23

Which of the following best describes The Adverse Possesion?

A) The sudden loss of land due to natural calamity like landslide
B) Giving up the property voluntarily to the government
C) A legal proceeding to divide a property owned by two or more people
D) A person who does not have legal title acquires legal ownership based on occupation of the land without the permission of its legal owner.

24

Termite is an insect living in large colonies with different castes, typically in a mound of cemented earth.

Which of the following may stop termites?

A) Chlordane
B) PCBs
C) DDT
D) None of the above

25

Real Estate Securities describe the securities of companies involved in a public trade that are engaged in the real estate industry.

Which of the following is required when selling real estate securities?

A) A Series 7 license
B) Registration with the state
C) A real estate agent license
D) All of these answers are correct.

26

A married couple decides to list their house for sale. The Husband meets with a Real Estate Representative and tells him that he and his wife would give her the listing. Husband signs the listing agreement.

Which of the following is the status of the listing agreement?

A) Void because all the owners of a property must sign on their listing agreements.
B) Valid because because it simply gives the broker the right to market the property.
C) It is illegal
D) Unenforceable

27

A **transfer tax** refers to a tax on the passing of property title to another person.

For which of the following are the transfer taxes usually the closing cost?

A) Closing Attorney
B) Buyer
C) Lender
D) Seller

28

Mortgage brokers help a client to find the best interest rates and terms for a mortgage. Mortagage brokers need to be licensed to work independently and legally.

Which of the following registers mortgage brokers?

A) Department of State
B) Department of Banking
C) Department of Brokerage
D) Department of Mortgage Brokerage

69

CONTINUE ▶

29

Two sisters, Mia and Isabella, own a property as joint tenants. Isabella decides to sell her share to a third person for a reduced amount.

Which of the following is the correct way to address the third person upon closing?

A) Joint tenant with Mia

B) Tenant in common with Mia

C) Tenant by the entirety with Mia

D) Tenant at will with Mia

30

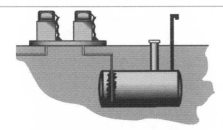

Which of the following is the foremost risk to the environment from underground storage tanks?

A) Wildlife can drink from the open ends

B) Toxic materials can leak from the ruptured tanks

C) There can be emission of fumes into the air from faulty vents

D) None of the above

31

Which of the following is the maximum age for a real estate salesperson/broker?

A) 18

B) 60

C) 65

D) None of the above

32

Which of the following is mandatory for mortgage brokers to disclose to loan applicants?

A) Net worth

B) Fees

C) Amount of credit line

D) All of the above

33

Lead-contaminated dust is one of the most common causes of **leadpoisoning**. The federal government banned the uses of lead-containing paints, but some states banned it even earlier.

When did federal lead-based paint disclosure laws go into effect?

A) 1977

B) 1994

C) 1995

D) 1996

34

Which of the following best describes an expressed agreement?

A) Binding on both parties

B) Written

C) Oral

D) All of the above

35

A lot that measures 840 foot in length and 670 foot in width was sold for $2,532,600.

Which of the following was the cost per square foot?

A) $2.50

B) $2.75

C) $4.25

D) $4.50

36

A **gross income multiplier** (GIM) is a rough measure of the value of an investment property that is obtained by dividing the property's sale price by its gross annual rental income.

Which of the following is the gross income multiplier of a house that rents for $1,400 each month and would sell for $150,000?

A) 0.009

B) 0.12

C) 8.92

D) 107.14

CONTINUE ▶

37

A **circuit breaker** automatically interrupts the flow of electric current when the current goes beyond a preset limit.

Which of the following is the use of a circuit breaker?

A) It distributes the electricity throughout a structure.

B) It muffles the braying of visiting in-laws.

C) It removes the moisture from wiring around bathroom areas.

D) It prevents water from leaking into an attic from the chimney opening.

38

If a property is worth $200,000 and an investor expects to be able to earn a net operating income of $11,000 a year, what is the cap rate?

A) 5.5%

B) 7.5%

C) 15.5%

D) 20.5%

39

Which of the following describes alienation?

A) To acquire alluvion through a court proceeding

B) To acquire property in an open, hostile, and continuous manner over time

C) The legal process involved in obtaining an easement by prescription

D) To transfer real property from one person to another

40

Mary has the right to use a path which crosses her neighbor's property to reach a public street.

Which of the following is the best description of her property right?

A) Easement

B) Equitable servitude

C) Restrictive covenant

D) Control

41

Which of the following refers to the outside rough surface of a frame structure placed over the studs?

A) Eaves

B) Molding

C) Paneling

D) Sheathing

42

The board of directors of a condo association is a form of a miniature government. The board members are elected by the condo owners to run the association and manage condominium property, which the board may do directly or by hiring a manager.

Which of the following is the frequency of their meeting?

A) Weekly

B) Monthly

C) Bi-monthly

D) Bi-annually

CONTINUE ▶

43

Net Operating Income (NOI) is used to analyze the real estate investments that generate income. It is equivalent to the total revenue from the property minus all reasonably necessary operating expenses.

A rental property brings in $600 a month in rent, and has annual net operating expenses of $3,700.

Which of the following is the correct Net Operating Income (NOI) of this property?

A) $2,000

B) $3,000

C) $3,500

D) None of these answers are correct

44

The Capitalization Rate, usually called **Cap Rate**, is computed based on ratio of the Net Operating Income (NOI) of a property to its asset value. So, for example, if a property was listed for $1,000,000 and generated an NOI of $100,000, then the cap rate would be $100,000/$1,000,000, or 10%.

Zion bought a rental property for $151,000. The property has a revenue of $18,000 a year and net operating expenses of $4,000 each year.

Which of the following is the property's cap rate?

A) 2.65%

B) 6.27%

C) 9.27%

D) 11.92%

CONTINUE ▶

SECTION 5

#	Answer	Topic	Subtopic	#	Answer	Topic	Subtopic	#	Answer	Topic	Subtopic	#	Answer	Topic	Subtopic
1	B	TD	SD1	12	A	TD	SD1	23	D	TA	SA3	34	D	TA	SA2
2	C	TA	SA4	13	B	TC	SC6	24	D	TC	SC3	35	D	TB	SB1
3	A	TA	SA6	14	A	TC	SC6	25	A	TC	SC6	36	C	TB	SB6
4	C	TC	SC6	15	A	TC	SC6	26	B	TA	SA2	37	A	TC	SC3
5	D	TC	SC6	16	D	TA	SA1	27	D	TC	SC1	38	A	TC	SC6
6	B	TC	SC2	17	B	TB	SB2	28	B	TB	SB4	39	D	TC	SC1
7	D	TB	SB1	18	A	TB	SB2	29	A	TA	SA2	40	A	TA	SA3
8	A	TC	SC6	19	D	TC	SC6	30	B	TC	SC3	41	D	TC	SC3
9	C	TC	SC6	20	C	TA	SA2	31	D	TA	SA1	42	B	TA	SA6
10	D	TB	SB6	21	D	TA	SA1	32	B	TB	SB4	43	C	TB	SB6
11	A	TD	SD1	22	D	TB	SB6	33	D	TC	SC3	44	C	TB	SB6

Topics & Subtopics

Code	Description	Code	Description
SA1	License Law	SC1	Deeds & Title Closing Costs
SA2	Law of Agency	SC2	The contract of sales and leases
SA3	Land Use & Regulations	SC3	Construction & Environmental Issues
SA4	Human Rights & Fair Housing	SC6	Real Estate Investment & Analysis
SA6	Condominiums & Suites	SD1	Taxes Assessment
SB1	Estates & Interests	TA	Rules & Regulations
SB2	Real Estate Finance	TB	Economics
SB4	Mortgage Brokerage	TC	Transactions & Processes
SB6	Income Approach to Real Estate Valuation	TD	Taxes & Insurance

CONTINUE ▶

TEST DIRECTION

DIRECTIONS

Read the questions carefully and then choose the ONE best answer to each question.

Be sure to allocate your time carefully so you are able to complete the entire test within the testing session. You may go back and review your answers at any time.

You may use any available space in your test booklet for scratch work.

Questions in this booklet are not actual test questions but they are the samples for commonly asked questions.

This test aims to cover all topics which may appear on the actual test. However some topics may not be covered.

Studying this booklet will be preparing you for the actual test. It will not guarantee improving your test score but it will help you pass your exam on the first attempt.

Some useful tips for answering multiple choice questions;

- Start with the questions that you can easily answer.

- Underline the keywords in the question.

- Be sure to read all the choices given.

- Watch for keywords such as NOT, always, only, all, never, completely.

- Do not forget to answer every question.

CONTINUE ▶

1

REITs (Real Estate Investment Trusts) are companies that own or finance income-producing real estates.

Which of the following is true of a Real Estate Investment Trust?

A) Shareholders receive profits from rent or mortgage payments.
B) The trust can only have one type of underlying investment.
C) REIT's can only be sold when a property is sold.
D) Each investor owns a specific property in the trust.

2

In an assignment, which of the following is the original tenant responsible for?

A) The assignee
B) The landlord
C) The managing agent
D) No one

3

The U.S. Government describes the **lead-based paint** as a paint or coating which contains lead in 0.5% by weight or equal to one milligram per square centimeter.

Which of the following statements is true?

A) The presence of lead paint in homes must always be disclosed.
B) The presence of lead paint in homes must never be disclosed if the home is being purchased using an FHA loan.
C) The presence of lead paint in homes must never be disclosed.
D) None of the above

4

Are Your Radon Levels Safe?

Radon is known as a naturally occurring radioactive gas which comes from the radioactive decay of uranium. It is usually found in igneous rock and soil, but in some cases, well water may also be a source of radon.

Which of the following is true for radon gas?

A) It is colorless
B) It is odorless
C) It is harmful
D) All of the above

77   CONTINUE ▶

5

Deed refers to a legal document that is signed and delivered such as the ownership of property or legal rights.

Which of the following is needed for a deed to be valid?

A) It must be in triplicate
B) It must be signed by the grantee
C) It must be signed by the grantor
D) All of the above

6

Which of the following refers to the state laws that protect investors from a lack of vetted information?

A) Blank Slate Laws
B) Blue Sky Laws
C) The Securities Act of 1933
D) None of these answers are correct.

7

A **septic tank** is a chamber usually underground where domestic wastewater flows for basic treatment.

Which of the following agencies requires to have well and septic systems?

A) Department of Taxation
B) State Department of Environmental Conservation
C) Department of Health
D) Environmental Protection Agency

8

Mutual assent refers to an agreement between two parties to form a contract. Mutual assents signify that the parties agree to the terms they are setting, as long as the requirements are in place.

Which of the following refers to mutual assent?

A) Fiduciary offer
B) Lawful objective
C) Meeting of the minds
D) Counteroffer

9

A **commercial lease** is for tenants using the property for commercial purposes such as business versus residential use.

At the end of a commercial lease, which of the following does the trade fixtures belong to?

A) Agent

B) Landlord

C) Tenant

D) None of the above

10

Which of the following is the best description of the discounted cash flow method?

A) A discount that is paid upon purchase since the seller guarantees cash flow

B) The ratio of the rent over the selling price of the dwelling

C) The sum of the present value of the rents over a specified period of time

D) The sum of the future value of rents over a specified period of time

11

Which of the following is true for a specific performance as a remedy granted by a court?

A) It voids the contract

B) It requires a party to a contract to perform on the contract

C) It requires a party to a contract to renegotiate the contract

D) It requires a party to a contract to pay a specific amount of money damages

12

A **prudent investment** is using the financial assets suitable for the risk and return profile and the time horizon of a given investor. Fiduciaries (such as financial advisors, CPAs, and others) entrusted with making prudent investments should ensure that an investment should make sense within the investor's overall portfolio and its fees should not detract significantly from the investment's returns. A good fiduciary should monitor the performance of the investments he has chosen for his clients, making sure that they are achieving their stated goals.

Which of the following should not be a prudent investment of a first time investor?

A) Vacant land

B) Thirty-unit suburban motel

C) Six-family residential building

D) Five-unit strip shopping center

CONTINUE ▶

13

The **income approach** is a real estate appraisal method that allows investors to estimate the property's value by taking the net operating income of the rent collected and dividing it by the capitalization rate.

Which of the following is a method in the income approach to property valuation?

A) Discounted cashflow
B) Direct capitalization
C) Gross income multiplier
D) All of these are correct

14

Management agreements state the specific development, administrative, and management services provided, and the corresponding compensation for the service.

Which of the following does a management agreement usually create?

A) A relationship of Universal Agency
B) A relationship of Special Agency
C) A relationship of Peculiar Agency
D) A relationship of General Agency

15

Closing refers to the last step in executing a real estate transaction which is set during the negotiation phase and usually takes several weeks after the offer is formally accepted.

Which of the following is not necessary at a closing?

A) Buyer
B) Deed
C) Listing Agent
D) Seller

16

Appraisal refers to the assessment of real property.

Which of the following approaches would most likely be used to appraise a school?

A) Cost approach
B) Income approach
C) Market approach
D) Smooth approach

17

Which of the following expenses are not included in calculating net operating income of a rental property?

A) Insurance

B) Mortgage interest

C) Property taxes

D) Utility Fees

18

An **open market** describes an economic system without barriers to free market activity.

Which of the following refers to the most probable price a property would be sold for on the open market?

A) Appraised value

B) Cost

C) Market Value

D) Seller's value

19

In investing, the **cash-on-cash return** refers to the ratio of annual before-tax cash flow to the total amount of cash invested. It is given in percentage and it is widely used to evaluate the cash flow from income-producing assets.

Which of the following is the cash-on-cash return of an investment having a $45,000 cash flow and a cash investment of $250,000?

A) 16%

B) 18%

C) 19%

D) 160%

20

Which of the following does a purchaser need to produce at the closing?

A) Certificate of Occupancy

B) Deed to the property

C) One year homeowner insurance policy

D) Tenant lease

21

If there is any triggering term in a closed-end credit advertisement, then there are three disclosures included in that advertisement which are as follows:

• The percentage or amount of the down payment;
• The terms of repayment; and
• The annual percentage rate

Which of the following requires accurate and sufficient information concerning the advertising of mortgage loans?

A) Duncan and Hill Decision
B) Federal Anti-trust legislation
C) Parol evidence rule
D) Regulation Z

22

A home with a market value of $420,000 has insurance for 80% of its market value. If the cost of insurance is $2.05 per $1,000 of insured value, what is the monthly cost of insurance for this home?

A) $688.8
B) $840.0
C) $861.0
D) $1,050

23

Dave wants to buy an investment for real estate wherein he can expect a cap rate of 8%.

Which of the following is the price of the real estate Dave wants to buy if the net operating income from the property is $9,000 per year?

A) $52,000
B) $78,000
C) $81,250
D) $112,500

24

The **HUD-1 Settlement Statement** was to itemize fees and services charged to the borrower by the broker or lender to apply for a loan for purchasing or refinancing real estate. HUD refers to the Department of Housing and Urban Development.

How long must the parties to a real estate closing be given on reviewing the HUD statement?

A) Three days
B) 24 hours
C) 12 hours
D) 3 hours

25

A **property tax** or also called **millage rate** is a tax on the value of a property levied by the governing authority of the jurisdiction in the location of the property.

Which of the following impacts does depreciation have on real estate taxation?

A) Depreciation lowers land value for local property taxes.
B) Depreciation lets the owner in taking a paper loss against the income of the property.
C) Depreciation refers to the total of all maintenance expenses associated with an aging house.
D) Depreciation adds up to the basis and is only essential for taxes when the property is sold.

26

Sam is thinking about buying a house. His friend suggests that he can approach the lender he knew since Sam is planning to have a loan to ensure he would be able to get the loan he wanted.

Which of the following does a pre-approval letter include?

A) Affidavit of an underwriter
B) An application that is under oath
C) Bonding of the borrowers
D) Verification of employment and credit history

27

A **regional mall** in the United States refers to a shopping mall designed to service a larger area than a conventional shopping mall.

Which of the following would a regional mall property manager give a high priority to when signing?

A) Jewelry retailers
B) Hair salon operators
C) Pretzel kiosks
D) Anchors

CONTINUE ▶

28

A **feasibility study** refers to an analysis of the success of a project's completion, accounting for factors like economic, technological, legal and scheduling. Project managers use feasibility studies to study the positive and negative outcomes of a project before investing.

Which of the following does a feasibility study in Real Estate determine?

A) The location for a successful investment

B) Whether or not the investment should be undertaken

C) The value of the investment

D) None of the above

29

Which of the following may compensate for a residential apartment building manager?

A) Kickbacks from maintenance service companies

B) Rebates from fuel oil suppliers

C) Percentage of rents collected

D) Key money; money paid to a landlord as an inducement by a person wishing to rent a property.

30

An **appurtenant easement** refers to the right to use adjoining property that transfers with the land.

Which of the following possesses an easement appurtenant?

A) Adjacent property owner

B) Former spouse

C) Former tenant

D) Upstairs tenant

31

Zoning laws in a town require an apartment building to provide three and a half parking spaces for every 1,000 square feet of inhabited space.

If a local apartment building in the town has 60,000 square feet of apartments, how many parking spaces should it have?

A) 120

B) 140

C) 180

D) 210

32

When you request a mortgage, lenders look for specific financial characteristics about you to decide whether or not you are in a credit risk?

What is used by financial institutions to determine loan amounts for borrowers?

A) Amortization tables

B) Apportionments

C) Quadrennial factors

D) Qualifying ratios

33

Which of the following considers a transaction where parents are selling to their son and daughter-in-law?

A) Valid

B) Recordable

C) Enforceable

D) An arm's length transaction

34

A buyer purchases a home for $4,500,000. He acquired a 30-year loan at 6.5% interest with a 20% down payment.

Which of the following is the amount of interest that the buyer needs to pay over the life of the loan?

A) $2,134,925

B) $4,677,984

C) $4,591,584

D) $4,321,125

35

Which of the following gives the correct formula for the rate of return?

A) (Investment Gain - Investment Cost) / Investment Cost

B) (Investment Gain -Investment Cost) / Investment Gain

C) (Investment Gain + Investment Cost) / Investment Cost

D) Investment Gain / Investment Cost

CONTINUE ▶

A **cash flow statement** refers to the financial statement showing the changes in balance sheet accounts and how income affects cash and cash equivalents, and breaks the analysis down to operating, investing and financing activities.

Which of the following is the correct formula for the total cash flow statement?

A) Operations Cash Statement + Tax Cash Statement + Financing Cash Statement

B) Operations Cash Statement + Purchase Cash Statement + Sale Cash Statement

C) Operations Cash Statement + Investing Cash Statement + Financing Cash Statement

D) Rental Cash Statement + Investing Cash Statement + Financing Cash Statement

Property management refers to the control, oversight, and operation of real estate. Management describes the need to be cared for, monitored and accounted for its useful life and condition.

Which of the following documents does a real estate broker prepare to obtain a property management job?

A) Financial statement

B) Property survey and deed analysis

C) Marketing Plan

D) Management proposal

38

An **easement** is a type of right given to an individual or entity to trespass upon or use land owned by somebody else. An easement is used for roads, for example, or given to utility companies for the right to bury cables or access utility lines. Landlocked homeowners sometimes pay for an easement to cross the land of another to reach their home.

Which of the following creates an easement in gross?

A) Utility company
B) Former owner
C) Sheriff
D) Current owner

39

Shiem is looking to buy a property that costs $115,000. The property can be rented for $750 per month. She has done her research and determined the net operating expenses to be $4,000 per year. Her desired cap rate is 6%.

Which of the following is the appraisal value of this property, rounded to the nearest dollar, using the income capitalization approach?

A) $34,000
B) $66,666
C) $83,333
D) $106,950

Which of the following refers to the only use
of lead plumbing pipes?

A) In the hot water tanks

B) For the incoming water lines

C) Conduits for electrical lines

D) None of the above

SECTION 6

#	Answer	Topic	Subtopic	#	Answer	Topic	Subtopic	#	Answer	Topic	Subtopic	#	Answer	Topic	Subtopic
1	A	TC	SC6	11	B	TC	SC2	21	D	TB	SB2	31	D	TC	SC5
2	D	TC	SC2	12	A	TB	SB5	22	A	TB	SB3	32	D	TB	SB2
3	A	TC	SC3	13	D	TB	SB6	23	D	TB	SB6	33	D	TC	SC4
4	D	TC	SC3	14	D	TC	SC5	24	B	TC	SC2	34	C	TB	SB1
5	C	TC	SC1	15	C	TC	SC1	25	B	TC	SC6	35	A	TC	SC6
6	B	TC	SC6	16	A	TC	SC4	26	D	TB	SB3	36	C	TC	SC6
7	C	TC	SC3	17	B	TC	SC6	27	D	TC	SC5	37	D	TC	SC5
8	C	TC	SC2	18	C	TC	SC4	28	B	TB	SB5	38	A	TB	SB1
9	C	TC	SC2	19	B	TB	SB5	29	C	TC	SC5	39	C	TB	SB6
10	C	TB	SB6	20	C	TC	SC1	30	A	TB	SB1	40	D	TC	SC3

Topics & Subtopics

Code	Description	Code	Description
SB1	Estates & Interests	SC3	Construction & Environmental Issues
SB2	Real Estate Finance	SC4	Valuation
SB3	Real Estate Math	SC5	Property Management
SB5	Commercial Investment	SC6	Real Estate Investment & Analysis
SB6	Income Approach to Real Estate Valuation	TB	Economics
SC1	Deeds & Title Closing Costs	TC	Transactions & Processes
SC2	The contract of sales and leases		

CONTINUE ▶

Made in the USA
Middletown, DE
05 November 2021